DORIS MILLER

DORIS MILLER

A Silent Medal of Honor

BY
VICKIE GAIL MILLER

EAKIN PRESS ★ Austin, Texas

FIRST EDITION

Copyright © 1997
By Vickie Gail Miller

Published in the United States of America
By Eakin Press
An Imprint of Sunbelt Media, Inc.
P.O. Drawer 90159
Austin, TX 78709-0159
email: eakinpub@sig.net

ALL RIGHTS RESERVED. No part of this book may be reproduced in any form without written permission from the publisher, except for brief passages included in a review appearing in a newspaper or magazine.

2 3 4 5 6 7 8 9

ISBN 1-57168-179-5

Library of Congress Cataloging-in-Publication Data

Miller, Vickie Gail.
 Doris Miller: a silent medal of honor / written by Vickie Gail Miller.
  p. cm.
 Includes bibliographical references and index.
 Summary: Presents a biography of Doris Miller, an African-American sailor from Waco, Texas, who survived the Japanese attack on Pearl Harbor in 1941, defended his ship, and rescued several crewmen.
 ISBN 1-57168-179-5
 1. Miller, Doris, 1919-1944. 2. World War, 1939-1945--Naval operations, American--Juvenile literature. 3. United States. Navy--Biography--Juvenile literature. 4. Heroes--United States--Biography--Juvenile literature. 5. Afro-American sailors--Biography--Juvenile literature. [1. Miller, Doris, 1919-1944. 2. Sailors. 3. Afro-American sailors. 4. United States. Navy--Biography. 5. Afro-Americans--Biography. 6. Heroes. 7. World War, 1939-1945--Naval operations.] I. Title.
D773.M52 1997
940.54'5973'092--dc21
[B]
                                97-32038
                                     CIP
                                      AC

*To my children, Leroy Ellis III,
Shamon Deondre Miller, Shanna Shaneke Miller,
Taya Shante Miller, and Malcolm Jamal Miller.*

*Forever I hold in my heart the heritage
of a family to be proud of:
Selvia Miller, my father, and his brother, Doris Miller
—true heroes, made by the strength of a great woman,
my grandmother, Mrs. Henrietta Miller.*

Doris Miller in May 1942, after being awarded the Navy Cross.

Contents

1.	A Strong Family	1
2.	Doris Makes His Entrance	8
3.	A Brotherly Foursome	13
4.	Life's Lessons	20
5.	Growing Up	27
6.	Doris Enlists in the U.S. Navy	35
7.	A Hero at Pearl Harbor	45
8.	The Navy Cross	53
9.	The Commissioning of the USS *Miller*	60
10.	Memories of A Cherished Home	69
11.	A Family Still Seeks Honor	74

Doris Miller being awarded the Navy Cross by Adm. Chester W. Nimitz, for his extraordinary devotion and valor on December 7, 1941. He was awarded the Medal of Honor May 7, 1942, and advanced to first class petty officer on June 1, 1942.

CHAPTER 1

 A STRONG FAMILY

The Miller family could be described as outrageous, tolerant, steadfast, and compelled to succeed by the force of their heritage. Strength, courage, and endurance have assisted them in their quest for survival.

As members of a family of nobility, each generation has reached for success in order to maintain that heredity. The struggles of life have been constant for them.

Henrietta Miller was born February 24, 1895, in a one-room shack, to West and Corena Murriel, in Riesel, Texas. A storm raged outside the tiny shack during her birth. The rain poured, splattering on the rooftop.

Luckily, the midwife had been present at Corena's side. Corena had been in labor for eighteen hours, aching and moaning with labor pains. The midwife had predicted a difficult labor, and it was. The birth of Corena's first child, Elcara, hadn't been a problem. But this experience made her reluctant to ever want to bear any more children.

The storm carried on for hours, adding to the mother's misery. Corena knew she would explode. Instead, small gaspy cries echoed in the room. Henrietta was born. There was no need to swat her on the rear to get her lungs opened up. She was doing fine on her own, breathing and screaming.

She was a plump and very light complexioned baby. Her father declared her to be as red as the devil. But he knew where the color came from. It ran mostly in Corena's bloodline. She was supposedly part Cherokee. West wasn't too dark complexioned himself.

It was a glorious moment. Another girl was added to their family. Although West had wanted a boy, he was satisfied with Henrietta. He had drooled with excitement throughout the labor, in hopes of a boy. With all that trouble, he just knew it was a boy. He wasn't displeased when he saw that the baby was a girl. But he said, "We'll wait and see next time."

There was no next time. Two girls were born to the union of West and Corena Murriel. The fact that Henrietta and Elcara were girls had no ill effects on their rearing or work tolerance. They were very capable work hands alongside their parents in the cotton and crop fields, as well as anywhere else.

The Emancipation Proclamation had ended slavery in the Confederate states on January 1,

1863. But it wasn't until ratification of the Thirteenth Amendment to the Constitution in 1865 that slavery was abolished. Henrietta was born thirty years later into hostility, tensions, and racial discrimination, the aftereffects of slavery.

Although social attitudes of hostility were evident, the ignorance was ignored. Henrietta and her family set out to succeed in a world surrounded with hatred because of skin color. Henrietta's parents were very stern in upholding the philosophy of God, which played a great part in her Christian beliefs. She accepted Christ into her life at an early age, and was very loyal in attending church services, along with her sister, Elcara.

That is how Henrietta met the love of her life, Connery Miller. They became acquainted one day during church services. Afterwards, Connery visited their home several times and became acquainted with the family. They were later married.

Four sons were born to this union: Selvia, Connery, Jr., Doris, and Arthur James.

Henrietta was a large woman, in height as well as stature. She was strong physically. Childbirth had no effect on her well-endowed body. She was healthy and well throughout each pregnancy. She gave birth one day, and was up and about the next day. Growing up through years of field work, sharecropping, and farming with her parents had hardened her to accommodate the ways of survival.

Her lifestyle with Connery was a reflection of the lifestyle lived by her parents. They worked very hard, sharecropping. Long hours were spent tending the fields, sometimes from early in the morning until late in the evening.

Henrietta's strength empowered her to succeed alongside her husband and to establish a foundation for their family.

Connery and Henrietta maintained a farm in Speegleville, a rural area on the outskirts of Waco, Texas. The structure of the house wasn't much in the beginning, but within time, they expanded it into a total of five rooms to accommodate the entire family. They glorified their dwelling and devoted much work toward its improvement. Yearly, they enlightened it with paint, from hoarded funds. They also kept it refinished with nails and boards—house, pens, sheds, the barn, fencing, and all. They whitewashed just about every board around them. An atmosphere of cleanliness was portrayed.

The Millers were not denied a place for relaxing, comfort, and ease after all their work was done. The family usually sat out on the porch, taking in a breath of fresh air and staring out over the pasture. They commended their surrounding success and talked about any repair work in store. The squeaky porch was due repairs. It was upheld by two wooden posts and squeaked when it was walked on. Connery promised to replace a couple of the boards to silence the squeak. He didn't do so until after the birth of Doris.

The family was always busy, but never too busy around the farm to watch out for snakes. They were a constant threat. Near their farm, a man had been bitten by a rattler and died before he could get medical help or properly treat himself. Connery had been bitten once, but had immediately tended to the wound. The family didn't rely much on doctors for medical attention. Mrs. Miller usually did the doctoring around the house, with old wive's remedies and treatments passed down from each generation. Connery had immediately cut the blood circulation off in his leg with a rag. Then he sucked the poison venom out, on the spot. He then went home to Mrs. Miller, where she properly treated the wound with one of her remedies.

The outside surroundings on their farm revealed their main means of survival. Cotton and corn crops, garden vegetables, and fruit trees overflowed in fields, receiving prompt harvesting in due time. The small, twenty-eight-acre farm stood out in an aura of glory. Chickens ran in all directions, flourishing off feed and ground surroundings, and were used for breeding, laying eggs, or providing food. There was a goat, a couple of cows, and a mass of hogs and pigs, along with several horses.

Henrietta marveled at flowers. The front of

her yard flourished with a variety of different kinds. She planted many of them from seed, and others were collected from out in the pastures, growing wild. She took many of them back to her house and replanted them, nourishing them back into the state they were in before she had removed them. She clipped off the heads of nonsurviving plants, dried them out, and replanted them the following year. A fence was built around the house to ward off any intrusion on her flower garden—man or predator.

Daily care was given in the spring and summer months toward the production of a blooming flower garden. Just as there was a scarecrow set up in the crop field, Mrs. Miller had one placed in her flower garden. It was smaller than the one in the crop field, but it was there. The flower garden scarecrow was adorned in the image of a woman, with a bonnet and dress. Connery teased his wife about it, saying it wouldn't scare away an insect, much less a predator. But it would surely scare away an intruding man.

Work on the farm wasn't easy. And their lives weren't comfortable. Hardship was endured although many long hours were spent toward a goal to survive. Regardless of production, there was a constant money problem, never enough to meet their means of living. The money earned from sharecropping was reinvested in feed, crop seed, food, and other essentials. There was never anything left over. After crop season, the money earned was reapplied into the system of farming.

Selvia and Connery, Jr., just couldn't understand why they were always poor, because crops and animals were always visible. Although Connery tried to explain the achieved goals behind their hard work, the boys couldn't understand. They saw no progress.

Looking beyond the flaws of hardship, together as a family they maintained their existence from meager earnings on their cotton and corn crops.

CHAPTER 2

 ## DORIS MAKES HIS ENTRANCE

Doris Miller was born on the small farm in Speegleville, October 12, 1919. The family's status was the same, scratching to make ends meet.

It was a chilly night when he entered the world, kicking and screaming like a siren. A smile smeared from ear to ear on Connery's face. He was proud that another boy was added to his family. He said, "Another hand in the fields, to help with some of this work around here."

"Well, I can see there's no problem with his lungs," stated the midwife, who delivered him. She was a friend of Henrietta's, and was well acquainted with the family.

Doris's cries were very alarming, a reminder of the hard labor Henrietta had. The pain had been excruciating, unlike any of her other children's births. She was constantly pampered and comforted by the midwife, as well as by Connery. Just as she was on the edge of defeat, with the feeling that she could not endure another moment of pain, the midwife soothed Henrietta with words of encouragement.

The mother was greatly relieved when Doris erupted. She teased, saying, "The little rascal just didn't want to be a part of this world! He was trying to hold out, and not be born."

Henrietta and Connery were content to have another family member. Yet, Henrietta had cherished the idea of producing a girl child to the family. It was something for which most mothers yearned.

When the midwife asked for a name for the baby boy, neither Henrietta nor Connery had one in mind. Henrietta was given the privilege to name him. It didn't take her very long to suggest a name—Doris. She said the name had a smooth sound to it, compared to the hard time he gave her during birth.

Connery was displeased with the name. He said it sounded feminine. Henrietta said the name was versatile. It could be for either sex. Connery continued to squabble in disagreement. He said that no son of his would be considered a woman, from the sound of his name. He said the name would knock on his masculinity. Regardless of his father's concern, Doris was given the name.

Many years later, Mrs. Miller admitted that she may have allowed the name because she yearned for a girl she would never have.

Doris was Henrietta and Connery's third son. Later, after the birth of Arthur James, their final accumulation was four sons. Selvia was the eldest, Connery, Jr., was next in line to Selvia, Doris came next, and Arthur James was the youngest.

The work around the farm proved to be unending. No one was idle, nor were there any exceptions to chores. As early as the boys were in diapers, toddling around, they were workaholics—a part of the work force. They emitted support to the family in the form of teamwork. The value of work was encouraged with a constant reminder from Connery: "If you don't work, you don't eat."

Food was one thing the family was certain not to go without. At mealtimes, the table was flooded with food. Henrietta cooked as if she were feeding an army. The four young flourishing boys, as well as Connery and Henrietta, had humongous appetites. Eating was one of their most pleasurable times. Adding to the boys' delight, Mrs. Miller baked tea cakes (their favorite), as well as a variety of cakes and pies.

Food provision wasn't a problem as long as there were crops in the field and animals on the farm. And they had both. At mealtime, when chicken was on the menu, three or four chickens were slaughtered, instead of one or two. When harvest times were poor, the family ate stored foods, canned and jarred. And when the meat supply was low, they resorted to stored meats, such as dried beef and smoked ham.

As young boys, Selvia and Connery, Jr., worked long, hard hours in the cotton fields. When they sought seclusion, the fields were also their hideout as they pretended to work, supposedly chopping weeds. At harvest time, the entire family was out in the field hurrying to get the job done.

The boys worked just as hard inside the house as they did outside. Mrs. Miller taught them to cook just about anything on the old wood stove. They learned to bake cakes and pies that were as good as Mrs. Miller's. And many times, they took it upon themselves to prepare the meals without any assistance. They helped with the mopping, scrubbing, and cleaning—even the sewing. No job was too good for the other one to do.

It was amazing, but with four boys, Mrs. Miller's house was kept clean. She taught them to keep everything in place. Even the drapes throughout the house were kept clean and ironed. She ironed the bed sheets, pillow cases, and even the underwear.

As toddlers, Doris and Arthur James tagged along in diapers, assisting in whatever they could do. There were many chores they were allowed to do. But there were some things that they did to which Mrs. Miller would put her foot down with a stern "no." This negative response was applied to messing with the wood stove, attempting to help cook, or playing around the hot iron when clothes were being pressed.

Many times, Doris and Arthur James were productive with their efforts. But a lot of times, they got in the way. Even so, Henrietta and Connery taught the older boys not to discourage them and, instead, to commend them with confidence. And confidence is what they needed. As a pack of two toddlers, they got into everything. Doris would spend frenzied moments attempting to put a sheet on the bed he shared with Arthur James. Afterwards, the sheet corners were always lop-sided. The entire household would laugh and snicker amongst themselves, but they never made themselves noticed. It wasn't until years later, after many efforts, that Doris learned the correct way to make a bed, tucking all four corners tightly.

Another one of Doris's challenging tasks as a toddler was attempting to mop the floors. He would leave more puddles of water on the floor than in the pail. The older boys ran behind Arthur James and Doris correcting mistakes, most of the time.

Mrs. Miller was proud of her sons, and commended them in an appreciative manner. She told them that one day they would make good husbands. A lot of giggling always trailed any statement about girls. None of them were interested in girls. It took them a while to develop to that stage.

CHAPTER 3

 # A BROTHERLY FOURSOME

Doris sucked on a bottle until he was almost five years old. He was Henrietta's most difficult child to wean away from the bottle. Regardless of how many times she took it away, she would end up giving it back. He was determined and persistent, screaming for hours. It wasn't until he no longer wanted it that the bottle was abolished.

Although Selvia and Connery, Jr., were constantly reminded by both parents to commend Doris and Arthur James for their efforts, they were caught many times bickering with them.

"What are you doing that for? You don't do it that way! I told you not to do that," the older boys would say. Sometimes the younger boys would storm away in tears. Other times they would ignore them.

When Mrs. Miller caught the older boys in one of their bashing acts, she reminded them with words of thought. "You fail to realize you are just a little bit older than they are. It took you time to get to where you are, so give them time."

When Selvia and Connery, Jr., were by themselves, they concluded, in a teasing manner, that Doris and Arthur James were more of a nuisance than a help.

As toddlers, Doris and Arthur James grew up closer together. Likewise, Selvia and Connery were close to each other. As they grew older, all the boys combined their closeness into a brotherly foursome.

One morning, Selvia and Connery, Jr., left to go fishing in the area creek. They had eaten chicken for two suppers straight, and wanted a change in menu. They told their mother they were bringing home some fish for supper. Some big ones at that. Mrs. Miller warned them to make sure they caught some bass. Bass was her favorite fish. Connery and the boys never could understand why she liked the fish with so many bones. But the older boys set out to catch some bass, along with catfish.

A fuss started to boil. Doris and Arthur James wanted to go too. Mrs. Miller disallowed them because she didn't trust them near the water. She said they were too young, and would be without adult supervision. They cried, fussed, and carried on whining, until she submitted. She allowed them to go, but made Selvia and Connery, Jr., promise to carefully supervise them. She knew that Selvia and Connery were good swimmers, and that Doris and Arthur James were not. She reminded them of that fact, and instructed them not to allow the young boys near the water's edge.

With those instructions in mind, they were on their way with two fishing rods and a bucket of worms. Their hands were locked tightly together, as they walked off down a trail. Once they were out of sight of the house, they unlocked hands and found rocks. As they went along, they threw rocks at different targets.

When they arrived at the creek, Selvia and Connery stood off a distance, whispering to each other. Doris and Arthur James stood at the water's edge, pointing at their shadowed reflections. Selvia and Connery crept up behind them, and pushed them into the creek. There was a loud scream, followed by a splash.

The older boys stood hitting at each other, howling with laughter. They watched the youngsters frantically swing their arms and kick. Doris and Arthur James both grabbed hold of a tree branch that extended from the creek bank. But the branch came loose from the ground, and they both slipped under the water. Within seconds, they emerged atop, gasping for breath.

After watching them flutter about in the water, attempting to swim without any real knowledge of how, Selvia and Connery decided to join them. They dove into the water. Doris and Arthur James quickly latched onto them, wrapping their legs and arms around them, soothing their fear.

The "rescuers" didn't retrieve them from the water. Instead, they tossed them around more so. It soon became fun. After hours of fun and laughter, Doris and Arthur James had learned to swim and were doing fine, without the crutch of their brothers. They had so much fun that, at the time of departure, they were fishless.

When they arrived home, Henrietta was disappointed they hadn't caught any fish. Her mouth savored for the taste of fish. Instead, that evening for supper, they ate chicken once again.

None of the boys dared to tell their parents about what had taken place that day on the creek. Their excuse of why they came home empty-handed was that the fish weren't biting.

Whenever Selvia and Connery, Jr., went off to fish after that, Doris and Arthur James were invited to tag along with them.

The boys were constantly reminded to avoid snakes, but they chose to seek them out. They would entrap them, smash them with rocks, or chop their heads off with a hoe. The fact that they might get snake-bitten, as Connery had been, wasn't considered. It was another challenging time of fun play. When Connery or Henrietta asked about a mangled snake, their response was that the snake came at them, and it was killed. This would set Henrietta and Connery off in alarm, going to war with snakes. They armed themselves with the rifle, sticks, shovels, and hoes, in search of snakes. The parents never did find one in the location the boys pointed out. But they continued to search.

Connery said, "Where there's one, there's more."

The work on the farm was constant, but the boys always found time to play. Many cherished moments had formed a bond, bringing them closer together. Just about everything they did was done together. They were outdoor boys, indulging many times in their most competitive play.

Football and baseball were two of their favorite sports. They did not only play amongst themselves, but with other kids in the area. They also found pleasure running around in the woods and bushes, hunting squirrels and rabbits. Fishing was enjoyable, as well as swimming in the creek, roaming the pasture, and chasing each other around the farm. When they couldn't occupy their time with anything else exciting to do, they indulged in a variety of "dare" games.

One particular game involved tracking down a skunk. There was no problem finding one. Skunks roamed the countryside, invading their corn crop. The boys would hide and wait. Once one was located, the boys dared each other to approach the skunk within a certain distance.

Selvia fell victim to this game many times, because he chose to test the quickness of the skunk. The game rule was to corner the skunk off to a standstill. Once the skunk stomped the ground, they were to disburse with quickness, to avoid getting sprayed with the foul-smelling liquid from under the skunk's tail. Instead of running off as soon as the skunk stood still and stomped, as the others did, Selvia did not. He waited until after the skunk had lifted its tail, which was, many times, too late. Selvia would taunt it, attempting to avoid each spray. After the skunk had given up and run off, or Selvia had been sprayed, he would go home content.

Once, after having been sprayed, Selvia went home with a smell that would kill an army. Doris and the boys rolled in laughter. They knew the truth. He told Connery and Henrietta, in defense of his condition, "I was working in the corn field, and a skunk attacked me for no reason, and sprayed me."

It was believed. Mrs. Miller was outraged at what she was told. And Connery went bailing out the door with his rifle, saying it was probably rabid, and he had to find it before it got dark. He returned sometime later, stressing that if any of them ever came in contact with an animal of vicious manner, to get away from it.

Meantime, Selvia had been ordered outside to undress and scrub from head to toe. Henrietta demanded that Connery find a solution to poison the skunk, fearing that the boys would go out and get attacked again. The stench on Selvia angered her even more.

Connery was fearful to put out any poison, saying it might kill off the rabbits as well—and that was a food supply. He said the boys just had to keep their distance from the skunks.

It was days before the scent was totally washed out of the clothing, as well as totally faded from Selvia. The skunk game wasn't played very often, because of the usual results. But it was an occasional challenge they endured.

CHAPTER 4

 LIFE'S LESSONS

Connery and Henrietta cherished each of their sons. They noted different personalities in each of them. Although their individualities in character differed, as well as their performances, they each enveloped a continuous energy flow, encouraged with mind power.

It was soon discovered that Selvia and Connery, Jr., were the sly ones. They got away with a lot of devilish acts. They were also very good at manipulating Arthur James and Doris to sway to their benefit, by donating or performing something to their liking. They were also the ones Connery and Henrietta considered "hard headed." They failed to listen to them many times, and misinterpreted many things told to them in the form of instruction. The older they became, the more trouble they got into around the house.

They were constantly drilled and programmed by Connery and Henrietta, who considered strappings as the last disciplinary resort. They held many logical conversations in an effort to steer them from their mischievous ways.

Doris and Arthur James weren't angels. They got into trouble around the house also, but they weren't as cunning and mischievous as Selvia and Connery, Jr.

Arthur James was a bookworm. He loved to read. He perceived and studied more knowledgeable subjects of interest. Connery and Henrietta were proud of his ability to learn. He talked to them, as well as his brothers, about things of interest, newly discovered.

At times, the boys would listen to him ramble away. Other times, they humorously debated or discouraged things he said to anger him. And it worked. They knew his weak spot. He had a temper that was easily riled. Selvia said Arthur James was very mind-oriented, concerned with many public, private, and worldly issues.

Doris told his parents that, at times, Arthur James sounded like a crazed philosopher. He said Arthur James was interested in education to the point of obsession. Despite these negative attitudes, Arthur James was not discouraged.

Connery and Henrietta encouraged Selvia, Connery, Jr., and Doris to conform to a stronger intellectual knowledge. Henrietta warned them that intellectual knowledge was one of the main crutches to survival, which they would surely need throughout life. She reminded them of how hard her life had been as a child, and how her parents and grandparents had suffered in the hardship of slavery. She stressed the importance of maturity in each generation.

Henrietta said that regardless of one's age, or the amount of knowledge stored in one's brain, a person should continue to strengthen his brain power; then they could have most things in life. In a dialogue to them, she stressed a motto she had learned through awareness:

> "Life's tolerance is a key to success. At times, life may appear manipulative and cunning. It is to be learned, it is a part of the burdens in life, inflicted upon us for our sins. That is why logic plays its role. And is a key, persisting beyond the point of reason, to success."

Each time the boys heard this repeated statement, it left them more confused. They would listen to her as though they understood what was said. But once they were amongst themselves, it was a ball of confusion. They argued and debated over different translations of her message.

One day, Doris asked the others, point blank, "Do you know what she's talking about?"

Selvia responded that if you sin, you're going to hell. They didn't believe Selvia. They sought a better answer. Arthur James told them the meaning was as simple as ABC. They should develop their brains, and endure more intellectual knowledge to survive, as well as be successful. Whether

Arthur James had given them the correct analysis or not, they accepted it. His explanation was easily accepted because he had endured many hours in learning, from books. Doris was just as determined to learn, explore, and succeed as his brother.

Doris attended school at Kimbleville Elementary, along with Arthur James. He wasn't as smart as Arthur James, but he made good grades.

Henrietta noted Doris to be an unpredictable character. He marveled at challenging situations. And his efforts always proved determined. Regardless of the action of performance or the way to achievement, Doris proved himself to be successful.

This portrayal of Doris's character was proven even during his infancy. As a fat, spunky baby, nourished off clabbered buttermilk and eggs, he was very clever. He proved to be steadfast and tolerant beyond frustration, in efforts to succeed at any task.

He spent frenzied hours attempting to grasp and maneuver a bottle to properly position it in his mouth. He wanted no assistance. When Mrs. Miller would offer assistance, by attempting to put the bottle into his mouth, he would scream and frantically knock it away. He would then strive to do it himself. The task of holding the bottle and putting it into his mouth was achieved a lot sooner than most babies.

One of the most favorite challenges for the

boys was "cornering a running chicken." It added to their humor to challenge Doris at this fun play, since he was a faster runner than the others. It was a show to remember, watching him trample the ground at such high rates of speed, becoming invisible within a distance, until he returned. The chicken would add to the show, fluttering and flapping its wings, in an attempt to avoid capture.

Regardless of the struggle, Doris maintained a gleeful smile as he held on to the chicken. If defeated, he revealed no manner of discouragement.

Mrs. Miller threatened to "skin their hides," many times, for running her chickens to death. She did not witness them at this game, but listened to their many conversations about the chases. Luckily, it wasn't a game played very often, or they would have been chickenless. The boys pretended to heed her advice. But whenever a chance arose, they took full advantage to sneak another one of the chickens off into their game.

These games of determination influenced Doris to be one who was never content, idle, or satisfied. He always sought a better way.

When the boys went hunting for squirrels and rabbits, they would usually use Connery's .22 rifle. Sometimes he put up a fuss over it, concerning the danger. Other times, he would entrust them to take it along, with a promise of safety and caution. They knew the danger of the rifle, so they never did anything outrageous with it. They never pointed it at each other, only at targets. They had witnessed it misfire more than once.

Hunting led Doris to a hobby in taxidermy. After the squirrels, rabbits or other creatures of the wild were killed, he would gut them of their flesh and stuff the carcass with dried straw. He would then pose them in a fixed live manner. Sometimes he mounted them to a wooden foundation, using nails, wire, and a strong bonding liquid. The more Doris practiced this hobby, the better he became. He even thought about taking it on as a form of living, later in life.

His family marveled at his craftsmanship ability. Although the animals were dead, they looked very much alive after Doris completed their transformation. Selvia and the others found it amusing, watching the animal carcasses after they were stuffed and posed. But they didn't find any real fun in stuffing the animals themselves. They thought Doris's hobby was nasty and disgusting. Doris posed and hung his carcass displays in many places throughout the house, as well as outside in the barn and shed house.

One time Connery, Jr., and Selvia took it upon themselves to cause a commotion by destroying several of the stuffed animals. They invaded the shed house, where he had placed several of his displays. As an act of mischief, they struck the stuffed animals with sticks, hollering that they were being invaded by wild animals. That caused a commotion in the shed house, as Doris stood witnessing their destruction. With his arms spread like an eagle, he charged them, taking them down to the ground. They punched, hit, and kicked each other for some time before the fight ended, with Selvia and Connery, Jr., holding Doris down. They finally limped out of the shed house with bruises and bloody noses.

Doris hadn't won the fight. But it was a tough one—a reminder to Connery and Selvia not to tamper with his prized displays. And they never did again.

CHAPTER 5

Growing Up

Although Mrs. Miller always cherished the idea of giving birth to a girl, she was unfortunate. This did not alter the chores performed by the boys. They participated in the washing and ironing, as they did with all the other chores.

They combed and styled Mrs. Miller's hair as well as she did. They experimented with different hairstyles. The boys teased that Doris wanted to become a hairstylist. He liked playing around with Henrietta's hairstyles, but he had no real intentions to be a stylist.

"Wash time" was a daily process. All the boys pitched in to line up three big wash tubs on a long bench. Water was then fetched from the well, and the tubs were filled. One tub was for washing the dirty laundry, one was for rinsing, and the last one was for "bluing" (a final rinsing process to brighten the clothes). The entire process usually lasted no longer than an hour—that is, if there were no water fights. Many times, they would splash water at each other from one tub to the other. And sometimes they would duck their heads into the water, to see who could hold their breath the longest.

After washing the clothes clean on the scrub board with a bar of their homemade lye soap, the boys rinsed, blue-rinsed, and then hung the clothes on the clothesline.

The soap used to wash the clothes was also used to scrub them clean at bathtime. It was their own specially made soap. Mrs. Miller added rose petals and perfume drops to a mixture of boiled pork fat and wood ashes. The scent stayed in the clothes, as well as on their bodies, leaving them pleasantly scented.

Doris learned early in life that pride had no limits. Mrs. Miller would remind them with encouraging words: "If you don't work, you don't eat. You don't eat, you die."

These same words were drilled in their younger days, and applied in their teen years. She often asked the logical question, "So where does the key to life lie?"

In response, they yelled, "In work."

Wash time was considered a fun process in comparison to the many other jobs enhancing their daily living. Those included plowing the crop fields, milking the goats and cows, collecting the crop, tending the horses, mules and cows, fetching daily foods for meals from the yard garden and crop field, slopping and cleaning the hog pens, cleaning the chicken coops, and repairing the house as well as the fencing. And there was a continuous flow of other chores. Connery and Henrietta upheld their children's welfare by these means.

The boys' actions and emotions were wayward, as with any other developing teenager. There were many times they were good, and many times they were bad. Although they got away with a lot of mischievous acts, many were addressed with some form of discipline.

One day, Mrs. Miller instructed the boys to chop the weeds and tall grasses from around the garden vegetables. They viewed the garden and decided the weeds weren't too big of a problem. They slipped by many times without chopping the weeds, until the grass grew a little higher. Then they went ahead and chopped it, making Connery and Henrietta believe they had been maintaining it all along.

Another day, Connery was away in town. Henrietta was in charge. The boys figured they didn't have to be too careful not to get caught playing around. They decided to go at it. Instead of being in the garden, they were out amongst the fruit trees, ducking and dodging, throwing fruit at each other. They were so involved in their play that they failed to notice the arrival of Connery. He was upset because a crop deal in town had gone sour.

Adding to his anger was the shock of what he witnessed. The boys, engaged in their fruit fight, attempted to run and hide, which was useless. Their father spotted them immediately. Connery was shocked and enraged as he examined the demolished fruit, splattered and squashed. Not to mention needlessly taken off the tree. He was furious.

He dug the boys out of their hiding places and marched them into the house. They were scared. They knew they were doomed. They huddled close to each other, but Connery made them disburse and line up in an orderly manner—the oldest, on down to the youngest.

Doris burst into tears. He denied any participation in the demolition. His cries played on Mrs. Miller's emotional sense, not Connery's. She was lenient to his cry and tried to convince Connery not to whip him. Connery upheld that they had all taken part, entitling them all to punishment.

Her sympathy was to no avail. Doris was whipped right along with the other boys. In turn, each one ran from the house screaming like a siren.

This strapping, along with many others, had somewhat of a controlling effect on their upbringing, but it did not put an end to the boys' mischief. They were determined to be boys—learning, enduring, and experimenting—regardless of the consequences.

When time was available, Henrietta indulged in sewing, as well as knitting and crocheting. They were talents learned from her mother. Henrietta made all her dresses, creating different designs. She also made many of the clothes Connery and the boys wore, including shirts, pants, and coveralls.

It was a talent Doris found very alluring. There were many days, instead of running around on the farm, that he chose to sit alongside Henrietta and knit. He knitted many of his clothes, including sweaters, shawls, and socks. He spent many precious moments to tailor these articles of clothing to perfection. Of course, Henrietta assisted with a few minor alterations.

Henrietta cherished an old foot pedal sewing machine. The boys teased that Doris sat at it as much as she did. Their teasing didn't bother him. Soon, they all joined in on the fun on the sewing machine, piecing quilts together. Henrietta taught them all to piece and design their own personal quilt.

Out of the many articles of clothing he made, Doris found it most difficult to sew coveralls. It wasn't that he couldn't make them. He said they were too time consuming. He left them to Mrs. Miller to make.

It wasn't very often that she made coveralls for Connery and the boys. But when she did, Doris was the most responsive in appreciation. He would put them on and do a little sly dance across the floor. The dance was composed of a body wiggle, in conjunction with a slide across the floor on the heels of his shoes.

Doris emitted his high-spirited mannerism and elated personality in his dance. His family knew to expect his famous dance each time he got a pair of new coveralls. It tickled them silly watching him dance. The others soon quit teasing him, and joined in mimicking his dance. They were all good dancers, but Doris was the show.

Doris was particular about keeping his coveralls clean. The other boys made fun of his finicky manner. Doris responded by saying all his clothes were entitled to due respect once they were put on his body.

Selvia said, "Yeah, like you're somebody really special."

In return, Doris said, "I will be someday." Doris converted his smile to a serious expression, and projected an image of defiance to succeed.

Despite all the activity on the farm, there was no corruption in organization. Mrs. Miller was an orderly person, programmed and set in her ways. The family's life functioned in accordance to days and time.

Henrietta was dedicated to serving Christ. She read her Bible daily, saying it was the key to salvation and a comfort to her soul, enforcing her inner strength. The hardship of farming and raising four boys required guidance. Her guidance was God. She said that without Him, her family would be lost in despair.

She enforced the rule that Sundays were days of worship in the Miller household. Although they did not all agree, it became understood. There was no washing, ironing, or just about any other work performed on that day. Although Connery's parents were Christians, he didn't show the same amount of dedication as Henrietta. It was somewhat of a debate whether he would attend Sunday services, or any church services. He argued and put up a commotion many times, saying he got his salvation at home, and he was tired. But most of the time, he gave into Henrietta's fussing and loaded into the wagon with the family. There were many Sundays that Henrietta, Connery, and the boys loaded into the wagon and set out en route to church.

One Sunday, Henrietta, Connery, and the boys were on their way to Sunday services. Henrietta and Connery were seated up front, indulged in conversation. Doris and Arthur James sat on the edge of the wagon's rear end, whereas Selvia and Connery, Jr., sat further up. The wagon reared as it was being coached up a hill by Connery.

There was a thump onto the ground, noticed by the back riders. Then there was a roar of laughter. Doris was out of the wagon, rolling down the hill. He grasped aimlessly, attempting to hold on to anything.

Henrietta screamed for Connery to stop the wagon. He didn't stop until he reached the top of the hill. He then yelled down to Doris, demanding him to scurry back up the hill in a hurry. The boys exploded in laughter as Doris scurried up the steep hill.

When he did reach the wagon, he babbled that either Connery, Jr., or Selvia pushed him out of the wagon. In defense, they stated that Doris had his legs hanging out of the wagon and fell out.

The parents knew it was impossible to conclude which one was the guilty one. One of them might have gotten an undeserved whipping.

The older the boys grew, the more conniving they became. And Connery concluded that the boys were becoming more resistant to whippings. He complained to Henrietta that they were getting stubborn and too big for a belt any longer.

CHAPTER 6

 # DORIS ENLISTS IN THE U.S. NAVY

The Miller boys grew to be strong young men. Although they were under their parents' scalps many times, their development was not altered in any manner. Each stood as a legacy of their parents; strong, tall, powerful, and perceptive. They all attended area schools, expanding their knowledge.

On many days during the first portion of the school year, they had to help harvest the crop in the field. After the harvest, and clearing of the field for a new season of planting, they went back to school. They managed to catch up with whatever they had missed, enabling them to keep up with their grade.

School was never intentionally missed. It was not only marveled at as a place to learn, but a place to engage in more activities with many of their peers. The boys were not shy. They were straightforward and determined. When peer pressure was encountered with classmates, it was not a discouragement to the Millers. Rather, it was an encouraging boost, enabling them to put forth more effort to be better people.

Doris was very talented as a teenager. Besides his abilities to cook, sew, iron, wash, clean house, and knit, he also mastered football, baseball, boxing, and loved to fish in the area creek and the Bosque River bottoms.

As a flourishing teenager, Doris stood five feet and ten inches, and weighed over two hundred pounds. He was very stout, with a muscular build. With this renowned stature, along with his athletic abilities, he won the position of fullback on Waco's A.J. Moore High School football team.

His coach noted him to be a talented player, with very quick actions. He portrayed a very clever style of defense, including tactics empowered by the strength of a bull. His far position allowed him to measure the opposite team's line of defense, before zooming in close on the play to knock his opponent cold. His hits were very powerful. Whenever he made contact with an opposing player, it was remembered. Doris never held back. His teammates called him "Raging Bull." He was never discouraged when a game was lost. He was more determined in the next game.

In an effort to help strengthen the family's financial stability, he found a part-time job after school. He worked in a small downtown restaurant as a short order cook on Austin Street. His work supplemented the family's monthly pay of fifty dollars.

Doris always sought a better plan for his future. He found no satisfaction continuing his education, and was determined not to devote his life as a short order cook. He wanted to advance in life.

Doris dropped out of high school at the beginning of his senior year in 1939. He told Mrs. Miller that he was beyond the age of schooling, and it was time he moved on in life to better himself.

He attempted to join the armed services, but was rejected because Connery and Henrietta refused to sign a waiver. They refused to release their son to the army, saying it might be the end of him. They reminded Doris that many men went off to war and were never heard from again. They dreaded that would happen to Doris. They did not relinquish their parental rights by signing the waiver. It was a decision that only Henrietta and Connery understood. They said it was for the love of their son.

Doris continued to strive to enter some type of military organization. He pursued the Civilian Conservation Corps, but was also rejected because Henrietta and Connery weren't receiving relief funds. Selvia teased him, saying that it wasn't meant for him to go anywhere. But Doris didn't hear him. He was very prospective.

At the age of nineteen, the opportunity came

along. A naval recruiting officer was visiting in Waco. Doris found the officer to be very convincing and persuasive with his literature on the awaiting challenges in the navy. Although he had been turned down by the armed services and the Civilian Conservation Corps, he didn't give up. Instead, he left his parents' farm and enlisted in the U.S. Navy, with no rejections. He enlisted at the Navy Recruiting Station in Dallas, Texas, on September 16, 1939.

All during Doris's life, he had been a fighter. He decided it was time he applied his fighting ability effectively, to fight for his country, in the navy.

It was a most memorable day for Mrs. Miller. Doris came home in a rapture of excitement. He broadcasted the news of his enlistment to the entire family. Mrs. Miller was overwhelmed with shock and disbelief. He informed them that he wasn't to leave right away, but had two weeks to spend with his family before departure. Mrs. Miller did her best to sway his mind. She reminded him of the warm family atmosphere he would miss away from home. And she told him that all the good home cooking would be replaced by mess foods, without proper nutrients.

She did a lot of talking to no avail. Doris reminded them all he had already enlisted. There was no turning back. If he failed to go in at the scheduled time, the navy would come after him.

Doris had no intentions to change his mind. He was determined to explore new and different challenges.

Connery chuckled, saying he'd be breaking his neck trying to get back home. Connery spoke in humor, but the sorrow in his heart reminded him of his seriousness. He was faced with the realization that his son had become a man, making his own decisions. And although it was hard to do, they concluded it was time they let him go to experience life on his own. Henrietta and Connery stood by their son's choice.

Mrs. Miller told him, "If the road gets rocky, you know where your home is."

When the day came to bid Doris goodbye, the family stood at the depot station with unending farewells. It was an emotional time. Tears were shed by all.

After many hugs, Doris boarded the train and was gone. At that moment, Mrs. Miller knew Doris was now the navy's son, not mama's boy. Her heart cried for Doris's awaiting adventures.

When Doris signed up, he had high expectations of seeing the world and exploring new and exciting fields. He was transferred to the Naval Training Station in Norfolk, Virginia. Although it was a challenge, Doris managed to successfully complete training at Norfolk, as mess attendant, third class. At the time of Doris's enlistment, there was a discrimination policy which limited the services of blacks. There weren't any tests for them, making it hard to advance.

Easing the tension of discrimination, the Selective Service Act was passed in September 1940. It provided for selectees to be introduced to training without bias to race. As a way of not having to comply with the law, the navy continued to rely on volunteers up until February 1943. Doris enlisted in 1939. The act was passed in 1940. As a result of the time discrepancy, and for some time afterwards, Doris didn't have an opportunity to rise beyond the rank of mess attendant. It wasn't until June 1, 1942, that more branches were opened to blacks.

Doris's enlistment meant hard work at menial jobs. He collected the officers' laundry, cleared tables, shined shoes, served food, made beds, cleaned and mopped floors. These duties were not new to him. He never had a problem doing his chores at home, and there was no problem with functional chores in the navy.

The navy made it clearly understood that blacks weren't allowed to handle guns aboard the ships. They possibly feared some type of uproar or retaliation—still aftereffects from slavery.

After completing training, Doris endured many changes in transfers. On November 29, 1939, he transferred to the USS *Pyro*, to await further transfer. He served as a mess attendant in ammunition, aboard ship *Pyro*. On January 2, 1940, he transferred to the battleship USS *West Virginia*. Within a short period of time, he was

Doris poses in front of schoolmates in his school days.

A photo sent to Mrs. Miller by Doris after he first enlisted in the navy at the age of nineteen.

Mrs. Henrietta Miller (left) in her earlier years. She poses with her husband, Connery Miller, and her sister, Elcara.

Doris Miller's grandmother, another powerful lady. Mrs. Corena Murriel was the mother of Mrs. Henrietta Miller.

Connery Miller, Jr., Doris' brother, after Doris' death.

Doris' brothers, Arthur James (left) and Selvia (right), posing with friends. They both enlisted in the U.S. Army. Selvia was the author's father.

Doris Miller, enlisted in the U.S. Navy, poses with a friend while on leave. Although he never married, loneliness played no part in his life.

Years after the death of Doris Miller, his mother, Mrs. Henrietta Miller, adores a portrait of Doris which hangs in the Doris Miller YMCA in East Waco. She is wearing the Navy Cross awarded to her son. Portrait by Leon Leonard.

Mrs. Miller stands on the steps of the Doris Miller YMCA in East Waco.

Mrs. Miller touring the Doris Miller Bachelor Enlisted Quarters, dedicated to the memory of Doris Miller, 1971.

Mrs. Henrietta Miller, after being shown a paper of recognition honoring Doris, shortly after his heroic act.

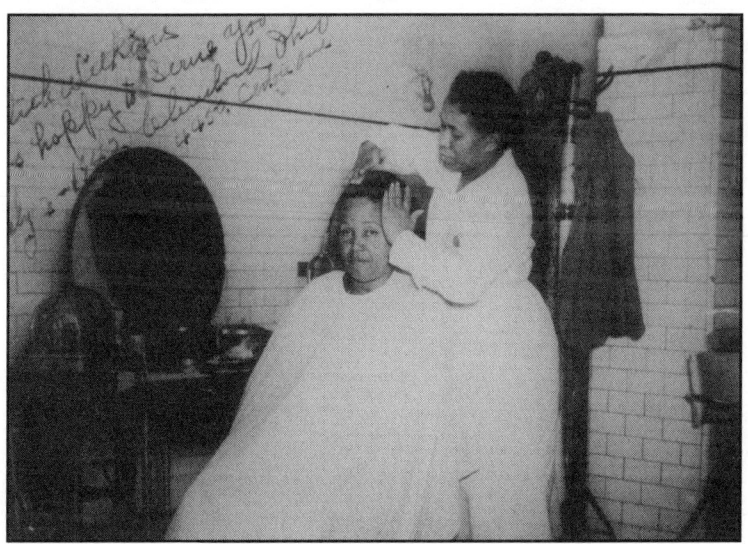

Mrs. Miller getting her hair styled by Edith Wilkins, in preparation for another event honoring Doris.

Mrs. Miller being escorted down the walkway of the USS Miller, after a tour by an electronic materials officer and other officers.

Aboard the USS Miller (DE-1091), Mrs. Miller was the ship's sponsor in the christening ceremony, June 1972. She is escorted by two navy lieutenants and Albert Bossier (middle), executive vice-president of production, Avondale Shipyards.

transferred back and forth aboard ships, like a rag doll being passed around. He was unable to stabilize himself. On June 22, 1940, he was transferred back to USS *West Virginia*. On July 1, 1940, he was transferred back to the USS *Nevada*. On August 3, 1940, he was again transferred to the USS *West Virginia*.

Throughout this period of being transferred from one ship to the other, Doris's efforts were rewarded. Regardless of the ship he was aboard, he adjusted to the surrounding environment, and gained reputable fame. He was liked by many shipmates. They boasted him to be an easygoing person, with a good personality.

One crew member warned, "Just don't make him mad."

Doris had a temper that wasn't easily elevated, but once it was riled, it wasn't easily calmed. Many times, when he was bothered or upset over a matter, he released his anger in boxing, with whomever his opponent was. Standing now at six feet, three inches, and two hundred and twenty-five pounds, he indulged in boxing aboard the ships. Doris was a very successful fighter. After many victories, he was finally decided as the USS *Virginia's* heavyweight boxing champion. And he upheld his reputation. His fists were like balls of steel, empowered with quickness and skill.

Doris's quietness puzzled the crew members. They couldn't figure him out, because he barely ever said anything.

A young reservist once asked him what force of energy empowered his fists.

He laughed slyly, saying, "A reminder of the fist of a powerful woman, my mother."

The reservist didn't take him serious, responding, "Yeah, sure."

Doris didn't care whether he believed him or not. He knew his mother was a fighter. Selvia had branded Doris as a replica of his mother. "One with very few words, and a lot of action."

Doris was such a big fellow and good boxer that the navy found his name didn't identify with their vision of him. He never had any real big problem with his name among his shipmates, with the exception of an occasional tease. But it was the navy's perception that the name "Doris" sounded feminine. They suggested he change his name to "Dorie," to uphold his masculine image.

Doris refused to give up his name—a name he so dearly cherished. He was never cowarded into shame because of his name, and felt it was nobody else's decision. He was proud of his name. It was a name he identified with, a reminder of home. He had already uprooted to be a part of the navy. He didn't choose to uproot his name.

To pacify the discrepancy over his name, it was recommended that he take on the nickname but retain his true name, "Doris." In the navy, "Dorie" became Doris's assumed name.

Doris was very supportive in the navy, upholding his duty as a seaman. As a petty officer, he put forth great energy to achieve his duties. He proved himself to be a devoted, hard-working officer. On February 16, 1941, his rating changed to mess attendant second class.

Doris got along with most of the crew. The atmosphere aboard the ship was mostly maintained in a family spirit. They indulged in recreational activities together, teased each other, and joked around. As reservists came aboard the ship from various training programs, they lacked the background of navy tradition. The new officers transmitted newer knowledge in functions of the navy, in comparison to the positioned officers' set ways of navy functions. Doris fell in place with both, the old and the new. His character was very likable, winning most of the crewmen's hearts.

Out of Doris's many jobs, he had one particular job that he found fun every morning. Each morning, it was his duty to arouse an ensign officer, with the exception of the officer's off day. Projecting the image of a prankster, it was a reminder of the fun he and his brothers had shared.

He would sneak up to the young reservist's bed and shake him with a rousing quickness. He would also utter some alarming words, bringing him to attention immediately. The words were very loud and commanding, throwing the officer into a state of stupor, in search of his whereabouts. Startled and dumfounded, the officer would throw a pillow at

Doris, or utter something humorous, once he realized his whereabouts. Doris teased the officer about being a sound sleeper. He told the officer that in the event of war, he would probably sleep on through it. The officer responded with a laugh.

Doris was soon warned by another officer that an enlisted man never touches an officer. Doris was warned it could lead to corporal punishment. Doris duly upheld the navy's policy. He wanted no drawbacks over a simple game of fun. So, Doris used another tactic, without touching the officer. He would sneak up to the reservist's bed, three inches from his ear, and yell at him to get up. He would then quickly flee the room, leaving the officer wide-eyed. The ensign officer never complained. It was an act of play cherished between the two of them. This fun play added to the humor aboard the ship, and distracted Doris from any loneliness.

Doris was ripe into the age of manhood. His interest in women had come with age. He was a handsome young man. On his leave time, he had his company of women. Young women were infatuated with his quiet, innocent, yet seductive manner. His looks and manner were very appealing. Although Doris never married, or was given the opportunity to establish a family of his own, loneliness in the navy played no part in his life.

CHAPTER 7

A HERO AT PEARL HARBOR

On December 7, 1941, on a Sunday morning, Japanese diplomatic representatives were meeting with the United States government in Washington, D.C. They were discussing ways to possibly settle differences between the two countries. No knowledge of the forthcoming war was evident. It was a sneak attack. Japanese planes were approaching the U.S. naval forces stationed at Pearl Harbor, on Oahu Island, Hawaii.

The naval base failed to identify several warnings of the approaching Japanese raid, which was a declaration of war upon the United States. Since the United States was yet maintaining diplomatic relations with Japan, American fleet and army units were not on a wartime alert. The United States forces were not prepared for the attack that lasted almost two hours.

At 7:55 A.M., the sun had just risen over the harbor in the Hawaii bay. Navy crewmen were going about their daily duties. The devastation began with sounds of horror. Japanese planes hummed as they zeroed in and destroyed the American army and navy planes on the ground. They then turned to torpedo and bomb the naval fleet units in the harbor. Within seconds, survivors of the Armed Forces were in defense. Men ran to their battle stations, manning weapons and returning fire.

The battleship *West Virginia* was there in port, along with seven other battleships. There were also cruisers, targets, and destroyer ships in port. Crewmen from each surviving ship put forth efforts of defense.

Doris Miller was aboard the battleship *West Virginia* (3B-48). He had just assisted in serving breakfast to the crew, and was working in the junior officer's wardroom, collecting laundry. A loud explosion, followed by a blast, quivered and shook the entire ship. It rocked back and forth. Doris was reared and thrown off balance.

At the onset of the action, the sounds led him to believe that there had been an explosion of some of the ship's equipment. But as the surrounding action proceeded, he knew it was more than that.

War had erupted in Pearl Harbor. The entire fleet was aware of the raid, and was scurrying to act in defense. The alarm for general quarters sounded aboard the *West Virginia,* piercing through the sounds of repeated blasts. It pronounced that Japanese raiders had struck Pearl Harbor. The battleship *West Virginia* was one of the first and hardest hit. There were six or seven torpedo hits and two bomb explosions. Sirens screamed, and crewmen scrambled to their battle stations.

There was another explosion. The USS *Arizona*'s forward powder magazine had exploded. Burning debris and flaming oil soared, splattering the entire decks of the USS *West Virginia*. Captain Bennion of the USS *Virginia* bellowed out instructions that all able-bodied men were to man their weapons and fire hoses. Doris regained his balance and raced to his battle station, which was the antiaircraft battery magazine amidships.

For a split second, fear crept in. Doris was startled, but thought to act quickly. He regained his self-control. He realized that he was in a real war, a situation completely different from the many months of drills. And already the Americans were in defeat. Torpedo damage had already rendered the battle station in total destruction. Doris viewed the horrid conditions as helpless.

The front part of the ship raged with huge, engulfing flames. Debris and twisted metal with sharp protruding edges were flung in all directions on deck. Amidst the ruin and destruction lay bodies of crewmen, sprawled over the entire deck. Men ran out amongst the flames in a confused state, only to fall dead. Some ran screaming engulfed in flames and jumped off the side of the ship. Some of the men ran around in shocked confusion. The Japanese planes shot down many of the fleeing seamen, with heavy machine-gun fire.

Doris's years of development would be rewarded. He quickly put his mind in gear to think beyond the destruction. His constellation of thought allowed his body and soul to jump into action quickly. Instead of leaping overboard as many of the crew members did, Doris viewed the conditions surrounding him and took control.

He spotted a crumpled idle figure sprawled on deck. Instead of abandoning this person, he jumped into an assisting effort. The fumes from the burning oils and gases were breathtaking. Almost choking from the fumes, Doris coughed continuously as he selflessly risked the bombing and strafing and began to carry the crumpled figure to a place of safety. He also aided other wounded crewmen from severely damaged areas on the ship. Along with the help of another officer, Frederick H. White, he hauled crewmen through water and oil to the quarterdeck. He then spotted his mortally wounded commanding officer, Captain Mervyn Sharp Bennion, lying in a pile of debris on deck.

A "flying shotgun," a field artillery projectile, had struck the captain in the stomach. Blood oozed from his wound as he muttered to Doris and a crewman to leave him and to save themselves. It was the only order Doris ever disobeyed in the navy.

With the assistance of Lieutenant Commander Doir C. Johnson, they lifted him out of the direct line of fire to a place of safety on deck. The assistant pharmacist, Leakand, bandaged the wound, in an effort to maintain the bleeding. The extent of the wound verified their decision. It was a hopeless cause. The captain was conscious and aware of the destruction of the ship almost up until the end of the rage, before he collapsed and died.

The ship was so badly hit that the starboard machine guns, which had to be positioned forward of the conning tower, had to be fired by one man holding up another, while ammunition was passed to the loader. Doris went on to assist with the ammunition. However, the heavy fire from the Japanese planes was defeating their efforts.

Doris was aware that blacks were prohibited from using machine guns. And he knew that he had no combat training. Shunning these negative thoughts, and overwhelmed with awe, he decided he could do better elsewhere. Observing the surrounding demolished conditions, courage pushed him into action. A dead gunner lay beside an unmanned machine gun. Doris moved the dead gunner aside and took over the machine gun. With aim and coordination, he began blasting away at the planes. He aimed at one Japanese plane and fired. His first round of rapid fire was a precise hit. The plane crashed into the harbor, plunging head first. It barely escaped the deck of the *West Virginia*.

While growing up on the farm, Doris's brothers had credited him as an excellent marksman. When they were out hunting rabbits, turkeys, squirrels, and other wild animals in the woods, "Doris rarely did miss his target," said his brother Selvia. "He was quite skilled. He was no amateur with a rifle."

Their daddy constantly fussed at them to leave his rifle alone. And now Doris was being rewarded for not having left a gun alone.

He surmised that the machine gun wasn't too big of a problem to handle. It was much like a rifle, but the machine gun had more firepower, a continuous rapid fire. Doris was a pro at just about any task. So aiming and firing the machine gun at his targets was no challenge to him. His main worry was getting bombed or shot.

A pernicious smile of enlightment prevailed upon Doris's face. He tracked them one after the other. With aim and precaution, he fired away at the attacking planes. He proved himself successful in the ordeal, as he watched the planes crash from his attacking fire. One set ablaze, spun out of control, and crashed into the water. It was a glory Doris marveled. An overpowering rage overtook him, permitting the actions of a furious fighter. For a moment he recalled the frenzied fury when he won his big fight as the *West Virginia*'s heavyweight boxer. Doris was ecstatic as more planes crashed from his fire as they zeroed in. He continued to fire, until he was ordered to abandon the bridge.

Doris was so juiced up with excitement, he was hesitant to abandon his conquest. But the order stood out. He abandoned the gun, dove overboard, and swam to shore.

It was a choice well made. He had abandoned the ship in due time. Fire gushed through the superstructure, and ammunition exploded everywhere. Many of the sailors who had stood in defense were also able to abandon the ship and swim to shore. Eight Japanese torpedoes sank the ship in forty feet of water, in the harbor bed. Doris had survived the devastating attack.

Isorok Yamamoto planned the Japanese raid on Pearl Harbor. He escaped, after achieving the successful, well-planned mission. There were 350 Japanese planes reported to be involved in the attack. Thirty-six were verified shot down, or failed to return to their carriers. Doris saw four crash before him as he fired. To uphold his proclaimed deed, he was credited with eyewitness accounts of fellow sailors to have shot down four Zero fighter Japanese planes.

That was Doris's first experience with a machine gun. He later stated that as he watched the Japanese planes diving in, firing away at the ship, it wasn't very hard to pull the trigger. "And she worked fine," he said. Doris was teased by the other sailors to be "the young Texan with deadly marksmanship."

The war rage carried on from 7:55 to 9:45 A.M. Doris estimated that he fired for about fifteen minutes. He stated that he had watched others practicing with the weapons before, but he had never practiced with them himself. He had no real knowledge of their power until the day of the attack. And his efforts proved successful.

CHAPTER 8

THE NAVY CROSS

It was sometime later that Connery and Henrietta heard the broadcast over the radio of the attack on Pearl Harbor. They also heard a report of a black sailor who had been very courageous in defending his country, by shooting down four Japanese planes. The moment the news was released, without any mention of a name as to who the "black sailor" was, Mrs. Miller knew immediately that it was Doris. It was her motherly intuition that led her heart to flutter with anticipation that it was her son who had been so heroic.

The phone at the Millers' house rang off the wall with inquiries, boasts, and brags of the sailor being Doris. Even before it was truly established that the sailor was Doris. Sometime later, within that month, a black newspaper, *The Pittsburgh Observer*, published Doris's name, along with his courageous actions. The world was now awakened to the courageous actions of a hero, Doris Miller.

The Miller family in Waco was on a rampage of excitement.

Doris Miller was a famed hero. Regardless, the navy was slow in acknowledging him. Reports of Doris's heroic efforts were first released by the navy, with the inferred description of a "Negro cook," who had aided his captain. They did not apply just credit, by failing to name him properly. But there could be no silence to cover up his deed to the public. Too many sailors aboard the ship had witnessed Doris's actions on the Day of Infamy, and they talked. His actions were highlighted by too many crewmen, constantly. There were many who boasted and bragged about his courageous actions and handling of the machine gun.

Finally, actions were taken to duly honor Doris. The secretary of the navy identified Doris by his name, and put a letter of commendation in his file. Doris also received a letter of commendation from Franklin D. Roosevelt. Although it was a step forward, the letter wasn't satisfactory to the public. The public outcry demanded more recognition. Various civil rights groups insisted upon Doris's acknowledgement, and stated that the navy should award him the Navy Cross. It was then that President Roosevelt upgraded Doris's decoration to the Navy Cross.

On May 7, 1942, Doris was awarded the Navy Cross (Medal of Honor) and advanced to first class petty officer on June 1, 1942. Fleet Admiral

Chester W. Nimitz personally presented the award to Doris for his extraordinary devotion and valor on December 7, 1941. The Navy Cross citation read:

> For distinguished devotion to duty, extraordinary courage and disregard for his own personal safety during the attack on the fleet in Pearl Harbor, Territory of Hawaii, by Japanese forces on 7th December, 1941. While at the side of captain on the bridge, MILLER, despite enemy strafing and bombing and in the face of a serious fire, assisted in moving his captain who had been mortally wounded, to a place of greater safety, and later manned and operated a machine gun directed at enemy Japanese attacking aircraft until ordered to leave the bridge.

The Navy Cross is the U.S. Navy's highest award. Doris's deed was the first recognized accomplishment for blacks in the navy. And Doris was the first black to receive the navy's highest decoration in World War II. The first official recognition went to Captain Colin P. Kelly, Jr., a white pilot who, on December 10, 1941, was credited with sinking the Japanese battleship *Haruna*. Doris shot down four Japanese planes on December 7, 1941, so truly he was the first full-fledged U.S. hero in World War II.

Doris was only twenty-two years old when he received this citation. His heroic deed disproved expressed thought that "blacks lack courage." His heroism also caused the navy to cease barring blacks from general duty.

Doris wrote home to his mother that after he

received the award, there was some jealousy among his fellow crew members. He didn't talk about the severity of the jealousy, or point any fingers. Mrs. Miller wrote him back some words of encouragement. She stressed that any individual in the public's eyes has to withstand a test of tolerance. She reminded him that because he was black, he would have to be more cautious. She said he would endure positive as well as negative aims. Regardless, she told him to be strong, and to uphold being the person that he was. It was a very inspiring letter. And when Doris returned home sometime later, he stressed to his mother how encouraging the letter was.

Doris also received other citations. He was awarded the American Defense Service Medal with Fleet Clasp, the Asiatic-Pacific Campaign Service Medal with two bronze stars, and the World War II Victory Medal. He was also eligible for the Good Conduct Medal for the period ending September 15, 1943.

Although Doris was not eligible to receive such training, he addressed a graduating class of noncommissioned officers at the navy's Great Lakes Training School. He then went to Bremerton, Washington, to receive training as a cook, one of his favorite talents.

In January 1943, Doris returned home a year after the attack on Pearl Harbor. His family hurrahed him for his well-accomplished efforts. He was also projected with pride throughout the city, and highly noted as a World War II hero in Waco, Texas. A ceremony was held in his honor. Doris told his family that it was God's protecting hands that prevented him from getting shot or blown to pieces. He assured Mrs. Miller that his daily prayers to God were not forgotten.

That was the most Doris mentioned to his mother and family members about the war. When asked for more details about the war, he commented by saying he wasn't supposed to talk about Pearl Harbor. His conversation was limited. He told them only what he wanted them to hear.

Mrs. Miller said, "Doris never did say too much about anything." She thought it was a reflection of his quiet, shy image—an image he had projected for years.

Selvia said, "It was a code of silence in the navy. That's why Doris didn't talk about the war. Mainly, because of what he did as a black man. He was getting too much publicity."

Mrs. Miller was in a highlight of excitement throughout this entire period. She toured the nation and attended ceremonies honoring Doris. She was respected as the proud parent of a heroic young man. Doris was highly publicized, and Mrs. Miller was highly acknowledged as well.

Doris had survived the devastating attack on Pearl Harbor. That was the most prized award cherished by his mother. She thanked God for the safe return of her son. In her daily prayers, she included a prayer for Doris. No amount of publicity, nor honors, outweighed Mrs. Miller's motherly compassion for the safety of her son. She pleaded to him not to return to the navy. As part of a mother's cherished instinct, she sought to protect him. She wanted him to remain home, there in Waco with his family.

But Doris was a determined individual. He was a man dedicated to upholding his honor as a navy officer and persisting alongside his fellow officers to serve his country. Once again, he departed to return to sea.

When Doris left again, he told his brother Selvia that he had no fear of dying, and to keep his fingers crossed that he would return home safely. The look in his eyes startled Mrs. Miller. It was a knowing look—as if he knew he would not return home.

After this historical event, Doris toured the U.S. promoting the sale of U.S. war bonds. Soon afterwards, he was assigned to sea duty on the USS *Indianapolis*. On May 15, 1943, he went on to the Naval Receiving Station at the Puget Sound Navy Yard, a naval shipyard. On June 1, 1943, his ratings changed to cook, third class. The exact date he was reported aboard the USS *Liscome Bay* is unknown, but in November 1943, in Astoria, Oregon, he was serving aboard the escort carrier USS *Liscome Bay* (CVE-56). He sailed to San Francisco, then on to Makin Island in the Central Pacific.

A day before Thanksgiving, at 5:13 A.M., the carrier was torpedoed and sunk in the Pacific Ocean by a Japanese submarine during an operation which led to the capture of the Gilbert Islands. The date was November 24, 1943. The ship had been commissioned for only three months. Doris was reported to have been killed in action along with the downing of the ship in the Pacific. Six hundred and forty-four shipmates aboard were also killed, along with the commanding officers, Admiral Mullinix and Captain Wiltsie.

CHAPTER 9

 THE COMMISSIONING OF THE USS *MILLER*

The Japanese admiral who had planned the Japanese attack on Pearl Harbor, Isoroku Yamamoto, was killed by American fighter planes on April 18, 1943, seven months before Doris's death. It was another victory fulfilled by the U.S. Navy in revenge for the attack on Pearl Harbor.

Admiral Chester Nimitz approved the American attack on Yamamoto. There were two Japanese bombers, one carrying Yamamoto and the other carrying his chief of staff, Vice Admiral Matome Ugaki. American bombers intercepted the Japanese bombers near the Solomon Islands and shot down both of them. Yamamoto was highly respected by Japan as well as by U.S. naval officers. His death was a courageous boost to Americans.

Mrs. Miller and her family never saw Doris again after his last visit, one year after the war at Pearl Harbor. Those last cherished moments with Doris continually brought Mrs. Miller to tears.

She recalled the infuriating day that the news of his death was released to her. A man came to her house and said that Doris was lost at sea, and presumed to be dead.

The news was striking to Mrs. Miller, inflicting a stabbing pain throughout her body. She cried a torrent of tears for the loss of her son, perished in the arms of the American navy. She assured herself as well as her family that Doris had paid the supreme sacrifice to save his country. The longing idea lingered for the return of that last hug shared between the two of them before his departure to sea duty. She wished she could have held him back from going. She wished she could have saved him. But the drastic realization haunted her. He was gone, and there was nothing she could do to bring him back.

Although Doris's body was never found, the 77th Congress validated his death, in compliance with Section 5 of Public Law 490. He was officially presumed dead on November 25, 1944, which was one day after he had been in missing status for twelve months.

Even with the awakening of Doris's heroism, segregation continued. Black mess personnel had disagreed with the navy's traditional policy of barring blacks from general duty. The navy's reason for the policy was stated to be, "For the interest of the navy, country, and blacks as well."

Doris's actions refuted this policy. His actions

released the cry for "blacks' right to fight." His actions truly interceded the racial barrier in the navy. The navy started opening doors to blacks that had been locked for generations. It wasn't until 1949 that the navy graduated its first black man, Ensign Wesley A. Brown.

Doris gave his life in the service of his country, in action against the enemy. He was posthumously awarded the Purple Heart Medal. Although he was deceased, Mrs. Miller was very honored to receive it for him.

Doris's heroic deed was an act which could never be forgotten, regardless of race or color. Many private and public institutions and facilities have been dedicated throughout the years to his memory.

A navy recruiting poster and a trophy awarded by the secretary of the navy, October 3, 1950, were among the many commemoratives to uphold this fact.

In 1950 a housing development was named in his honor, in Corona, New York.

In 1951 a Doris Miller Foundation Trophy was displayed in the Pentagon in Washington, D.C., as a memento of Doris. The foundation was established in 1947 by a group of Chicago citizens. Annually, the trophy is awarded to an outstanding individual or organization in the field of race relations and civic enterprise.

Waco and Dallas were not remiss in honoring Doris. They had a celebration highlighting that he was a native Texan of the two cities. The cities respected and honored him as an unselfish man, who contributed of himself to honor his country.

On December 7, 1971, the Service School Command Naval Training Center in Great Lake, Illinois, commemorated and gave honor to his heroism. Mrs. Miller, at the age of seventy-six, along with her son Arthur James, attended the dedication ceremony. In remembrance of Doris, a part of the Naval Training Center was dedicated and named Doris Miller Bachelor Enlisted Quarters. The school's structural aim was to promote black sailors to work in specialized jobs as petty officers—another step forward for blacks.

Mrs. Miller was overwhelmed to attend the dedication ceremony in honor of her son. Throughout the entire program, tears twinkled down her cheeks as she recollected memories of a fine son, Doris. It was once again a reminder he was not forgotten in the eyes of America.

Printed in the dedication program was an inscription highlighting Doris's bravery. The inscription upheld Doris's actions to be courageous and stated that his actions were portraits of an efficient American navy.

The navy announced that a new destroyer escort ship was under construction at the Avondale Shipyard, a naval shipyard in West Wego, Louisiana. The navy stated that because of Doris's distinguished devotion at Pearl Harbor, the ship would be named for him. Mrs. Miller was very proud to hear the news of the new ship, and the honor of the navy, once again, to Doris.

On June 3, 1972, the U.S. Navy named the destroyer escort after Doris Miller: Ocean Escort USS *Miller* (DE-1091). The ship was commissioned June 30, 1973.

The ship's insignia represented "The Arms of *Miller*," which contributed themes reflecting Doris's life and family. This highly individualized Maltese Cross suggests the Navy Cross won by Petty Officer Doris Miller at Pearl Harbor.

The symbol depicts the task and ferocity of a modern naval warship. Within the basic unit of the ship's insignia lies a circle. The circle signifies unity, the most appropriate device with which to express the feeling and concept of "one navy." The ship is named after a black American, typifying that spirit of unity, without prejudice. The sunburst surrounding the circle represents the constant alertness and vigil required of the navy.

The gold color of the insignia symbolizes the courage and bravery displayed by Doris Miller during the Japanese attack on Pearl Harbor. The four arms stemming from the inner circle area each display a white triangle to symbolize the four cardinal points of the compass. This arrangement represents the presence of naval warships at the four corners of the globe. The blue color of the cross represents the sea and sky, and loyalty.

The Trident of Neptune lies within the circle. It is a symbol which for years has stood for naval tradition and heritage. The furious, three-headed serpent-tailed dog of Greek mythology, Cerberus, was a guardian in ancient times. So was Miller depicted, as a guardian. Cerberus's three headedness is especially appropriate: Three wolves' heads were displayed on the Miller coat of arms. The Cerberus figure is oriented to watch over three warfare areas: air, surface, and subsurface. The motto "Courage–Devotion" was derived from the citation awarded to Doris Miller for his heroism on the outstanding "Day of Infamy," December 7, 1941.

The USS *Miller* was one of the most versatile ships afloat. She was the fourteenth ship of the Joseph Hewew class of ocean escorts. The ship's main purpose was to locate and destroy enemy submarines. But it was also capable of forming other missions, such as patrol, blockade, and shore bombardment, surveillance, search and rescue, and antiwar warfare. The USS *Miller* was built in the reflection of a great man, Doris Miller.

Doris's father had lived to witness his son's heroic deed. It was a short time afterwards that he fell victim and succumbed to a stroke. Mrs. Miller continued to carry on in a courageously proud manner, with her remaining three sons by her side.

The naming of the USS *Miller* was an honor that would be celebrated with a commissioning ceremony. It was yet another glorious time when Mrs. Miller received notice that she was chosen sponsor for the ceremony. She was very proud to be this special person. The navy would fly Mrs. Miller and her family to the ceremony.

Mrs. Miller was accompanied to the ceremony by her sister, Mrs. Elcara Woods, "Matron of Honor," and her son, Arthur James Miller. Selvia didn't attend. He was one who never did like being in the public eye too much.

As sponsor, Mrs. Miller received a traditional bouquet of flowers at the launching site. She understood that by christening the USS *Miller*, she would forever hold a special place among those who manned the ship. Evolved from pagan rituals, the belief was that the sponsor's spirit entered the ship at the time of launching and would remain there forever.

Christening and launching ceremonies for seagoing ships and boats is a practice of all nations in the world. Its origin goes back at least 4,000 years. A bottle of wine, brandy, or Irish whiskey was usually broken over the bow of the ship. This practice also derived from pagan rituals, contrived to ward off evil spirits and dangers of the sea.

The *Concord* was the first U.S. Navy ship to be launched, in 1828. The sponsor's name has been lost in history. Although the sponsor began this powerful tradition, she is only remembered as "a young lady of Portsmouth." Since her performance, male sponsors have been extremely rare. Champagne is now the standard christening medium.

Mrs. Miller was ecstatic as she smashed the traditional bottle of champagne across the bow of the *Miller* (DE-1091). Tears of excitement rolled down her cheeks as the bottle splattered with a bang, and the glittering champagne poured out into the waters. A split second image of Doris's face flashed before her eyes, as she endured the memorable thrill. She thought the image of Doris's face to be a product of her imagination. Whether it was her mind playing tricks on her or not, she called the expression on his face an enlightened smile of content.

A highlight of this ceremony was the speech made by the Honorable Barbara Jordan, a powerful black congresswoman from Texas. She said that black people struggle to win equal or full rights as American citizens, whereas people like Doris have fought hard just to protect rights of *all* people. Also in her speech was the message that the navy was shaking past prejudices, and making equality a reality in America.

After the official party departed, the ship was then open to general visiting.

There were many letters of recognition to the captain of the USS *Miller*, in regards to the awakening of the ship. The letters were addressed to Lieutenant Commander Lynn P. Blasch. Many high officials paid tribute in the form of a letter. Among them was a letter from the chief of naval operations. He spoke highly of Doris's heroism and the symbology of the USS *Miller*.

He stressed that the ship was designed to do many jobs well, coinciding with Doris's heroic acts. He signified that Doris's fighting spirit led him to disregard bombs and bullets, and fire back at the enemy. He wrote that Doris then gave his life in action during the operation which led to the capture of Tarawa. In his opinion Doris's actions exemplified the courage and humanity which have always been hallmarks of the American sailor. He was sure that Captain Blasch and his crew would exemplify the same qualities.

The christening of the ship was not only an honor to Doris. It was also a tribute to American history.

Since the day her commission pennant was broken, USS *Miller* became the responsibility of her captain and crew. Her personality and soul were instilled by the men who served her. The will, spirit, and dedication of these men made her and kept her ready for whatever she was called upon to do, in war and in peace.

CHAPTER 10

 # MEMORIES OF A CHERISHED HOME

Although Mrs. Miller's sons were young adults, she was there to aid in their guidance and support during the exploitation of Doris. Her mother, Corena Murriel, moved in with Henrietta and her family. Corena's husband was deceased and she was alone. Sometime later, Connery died. With a combination of learned knowledge and instinct, the two women strengthened their endurance and supported each other.

The Millers vacated their first home shortly after Doris went off to the navy, in search of a bigger one. Shortly afterwards the suburb area was flooded out, to make way for Lake Waco. Doris's birth site now lies somewhere in Lake Waco. Just as Doris's death site was in water, his birth site is underwater too. As such, there is no official memorial site for his birth or a final resting place.

The Millers found residency in a lovely home in Waco at 1213 Southey Avenue. It was their dream come true. In comparison to their first home, it was much roomier. Mrs. Miller was able to purchase the house with hoarded savings, accumulated on the farm. Once she was established there, she contributed to its payment by baking and selling cakes and pies. Area neighbors complimented her cakes and pies to be very tasty—"mouth watering," as one woman put it. She said that after she bought one and ate it, she couldn't wait to get her hands on another one.

The Millers also acquired money from the sale of wild rabbits, eggs, and chickens. They hunted the rabbits and raised the chickens. The family had no problem surviving. They had the strength, knowledge, and willpower, and it was applied effectively.

Doris never did enjoy the privilege to live at 1213 Southey, but his family cherished his belongings. They took many of his personal belongings, as well as medals and awards, and displayed them in a keepsake place in their home. These things were all Mrs. Miller had by which to cling to Doris. She cherished them dearly.

Mrs. Miller purchased a lot adjacent to her home and planted crops there. The field was tilled, planted, and harvested seasonally—the exact process performed on the farm in Speegleville.

A mysterious fire erupted in the Millers' home in 1957. The home was engulfed in flames, partially charred and smoked, but not totally destroyed. Most of the medals awarded to Doris were destroyed. There was an immediate response from the public to help reestablish their home. The home was rebuilt, modernizing it more so. And a ceremony was held in the city of Waco to replace most of the medals that Doris had won in World War II. Congressman W. R. Poage of Waco secured duplicates of the medals. The ceremony was held at the Doris Miller YMCA, in East Waco, and duplicated medals were presented to Mrs. Miller and her family. She received duplicates of the Navy Cross, the Purple Heart, a Good Conduct Medal, an American Defense Service Medal with Fleet Clasp, Asiatic–Pacific Campaign Service Medal, and World War II Medal.

Arthur James accompanied Mrs. Miller to the ceremony. The local naval reserve commander was present to represent the navy. Dr. G. H. Radford, a black city councilman, presented Mrs. Miller with another award, which she was very pleased to receive. He presented a "Doris Miller Day" proclamation. Once again Mrs. Miller was overwhelmed.

Mrs. Miller and her family were continually uplifted with highlights of the Doris Miller story, which were very much appreciated. The family remained strong.

In her late stage in life, Corena was feeble, but her words were stern and very powerful. Her most encouraging words to her daughter were:

"Hold your head up and stand strong on the

ground you walk on. You have every reason to be proud. Not only because of who you are, but for your blessings as well. Praise and thank God every day of your life."

Those words were very inspiring and they lingered with Mrs. Miller throughout the remainder of her life. Corena remained there in residence with Henrietta until her departure peacefully one night, in her sleep.

Connery, Jr., Selvia, and Arthur James each served in the U.S. Army. They were drafted shortly after Doris's enlistment. Although they were strong young men, they were also "mama's boys." No matter where they went, what they did, who they were involved with, or how long they stayed away, they always ended up back at mama's house. Connery, Jr., married, and was the father of seven children. In the final stages of a lengthy illness he moved back home with Mrs. Miller. She was by his side each and every day until he died.

Arthur James became a schoolteacher, and also married a schoolteacher. They raised one daughter. Mrs. Miller always maintained a room in her home for Arthur James, as she did for Selvia also.

Selvia was an adventurous type fellow. He married more than once, and was finally content to settle down in marriage with Irene Washington. To this union, seven children were born (Brende, Henrietta, Florietta, Vickie, Selvia, Jr., Janice, and Gerald Wayne).

Mrs. Miller's philosophy of life was well bestowed to her many grandchildren. There were cherished memories endured at 1213 Southey Avenue.

Mrs. Miller's strong, stern, and unselfish ways projected a content lifestyle. Doris's disciplined morals, courageous spirit, and respect for humanity were learned influences from a powerful woman.

Mrs. Miller had lost a husband, mother, and two sons, all within a flash of time. The hurt was beyond the torment of pain. But she went forward, with that awakened knowledge that she was Mrs. Henrietta Miller, the proud mother of four sons—one being a hero of fame, Doris Miller. She was relieved that her son Doris stood out in fame. She knew that Doris's contribution to America's history was strengthening, and a step forward for blacks.

CHAPTER 11

 A FAMILY STILL SEEKS HONOR

Mrs. Miller recalled a day when a movie producer's agent came to her house with an offer. He wanted to feature Doris's story in a movie. It had been years since his death. Mrs. Miller was elated that Doris's heroic efforts were yet unforgotten in the eyes of America, and would be highlighted in a movie.

However, their offer was based on the condition that Doris be portrayed as a white man, rather than a black man. Mrs. Miller refused to accept the agreement. She said that if Doris couldn't be portrayed as who he was, as a black man, then there would be no movie representing Doris.

She said her son hadn't chosen a race to defend. He fought for his country, America—a country of all colors.

Years later, there was another proposition for the making of a film on Doris. This time there was discrepancy in selection of an actor to portray the image, physique, and character of Doris. Mrs. Miller was unsure of whether she signed anything, agreeing to the portrayal of her son in a movie. She was getting up into age, and found many important matters to be confusing. She stated that Arthur James handled most of her business and may have given the producers the go ahead with the selected actor who portrayed Doris in the made-for-television movie.

In the 20th Century-Fox motion picture entitled *"Tora! Tora! Tora!,"* Doris's heroism was displayed very briefly at the beginning of the film. His role was played by a black actor, Elven Havard. Although Doris's actions were credited in the movie, the portrayal somewhat diminished Doris's credit, in comparison to his true actions on the Day of Infamy. Doris exhibited more action in the two-hour attack on Pearl Harbor aboard the USS *West Virginia* than the brief time portrayed in the movie.

Mrs. Miller was not only burdened with this type treatment from the movie world. She was burdened with the same respect from Congress.

Doris never received the Congressional Medal of Honor, the nation's highest military award for bravery in combat in World Wars I and II. About 1.5 million black Americans fought in World Wars I and II. No blacks received the Medal of Honor.

Doris, as a black man, was considered to have aided in breaking the racial barrier in the navy.

He gave of himself, not just for black Americans but all Americans. Congress awarded a Congressional Medal of Honor to 549 men in World Wars I and II. Mrs. Miller wondered why it was so difficult to award it to one more, a black man, who also fought and died for his country.

As time passed, Mrs. Miller was drawn to her belief that the treatment of Doris was racism. She became ill in the 1980s and was forced to leave her home because of medical reasons. Having to abandon her home was another tragedy she endured. She had rooted her life into that home.

She moved to Midland, Texas, and resided at the home of Selvia's oldest daughter. The many years of loving care and attention she had given were returned to her there.

Mrs. Miller's pain was unending. And she still hurt with Congress' lack of acknowledgment to Doris, right up to the bitter end. She died of cancer in June of 1982. Her remains were transported back to her hometown, Waco, where she was laid to rest in the Doris Miller Cemetery, along with her husband and other perished family members.

Years later, cancer struck again. Both Selvia and Arthur James would die of the disease. They were the last of that generation of Millers. Their absence reflects no lack of acknowledgment for Doris. Mrs. Miller's cry for the Congressional Medal of Honor is continually revived and voiced through others.

It is not a cry for public sentiment, but a cry

for Doris to be honored in accordance to his citizenship.

Politicians did begin a movement to persuade the U.S. Department of Defense to award a posthumous Congressional Medal of Honor to Doris. House resolutions to endorse the Medal of Honor for Doris were also introduced. The U.S. Navy responded by saying the five-year limitation to awards expired years ago. The Congressional Medal of Honor, however, is awarded through the actions of Congress, not the navy.

Ever since the criticism of Congress for ignoring Doris Miller, his fame has been endangered.

As of 1988, the destroyer escort USS *Miller*, named after Doris in 1977, was home ported in Newport, Rhode Island. It was suddenly decommissioned in 1991.

In television accounts of the 49th anniversary of the December 7, 1941, attack at Pearl Harbor, Doris was not noted.

On the 50th anniversary, some major television networks broadcast special programs on the attack at Pearl Harbor. Again, Doris was ignored.

Regardless of these oversights, Doris is recognized throughout the United States. The Doris Miller YMCA, in East Waco, bears a historical marker in his honor. The marker highlights Doris Miller as being the first black man to receive the Navy Cross.

Other places named after him include the Doris Miller Cemetery, near Bellmead, the

Bledsoe-Miller Park in Waco, several schools in Houston and Philadelphia, an auditorium in Rosewood Park, at Austin, Texas, a VFW post in Los Angeles, and the Doris Miller Foundation in Chicago.

In 1994 a new elementary magnet school in Waco was renamed after Doris Miller. A local recreation center and a day care center also bear his name in Waco.

In 1970, located at the Naval Air Station, Chase Field, in Beeville, Texas, the Dining Hall was opened and named for Doris.

The Doris Miller Monument, made of polished red marble and granite, stands almost eight feet tall at the Veteran's Administration Medical Center in Waco. It was dedicated in 1984.

His name is continually highlighted in ceremonies. In remembrance of Doris, a ceremony was held in Waco on December 4, 1994—fifty-three years after Doris's heroic actions. The Central Texas Branch of the Association for the Study of Afro-American Life and History sponsored the event at the Helen Marie Taylor Museum. It was stressed that Miller was a native of Waco who died a World War II hero. It was stated that regardless of color or ethnic background, we, as a nation, should care for each other.

Mrs. Miller's home at 1213 Southey was vacated for some time. There had been a problem with renting it, with reports of strange, ghost-like sightings, even by family members. It was abandoned and left in a deteriorating state. The house was soon red-tagged by the city of Waco. The red tag meant that no one could live there until the house was repaired to meet city standards.

Arthur James had planned to maintain the house as an exhibit center in memory of Doris, as well as out of respect for Mrs. Miller. It was estimated that the price of restoration and conversion of the home into a memorial would be around $50,000. Arthur James was striving for assistance, along with historians, toward the cause. Before any results were established, Arthur James died.

On December 7, 1989, Waco city officials approved the demolition of the Miller home. The order was approved on the very same day of Doris's heroic deed in 1941.

The controversy over the Congressional Medal of Honor continues. It is stipulated that in order for Doris to receive the Congressional Medal of Honor, his recognition has to proceed in this chain of order: the president, secretary of defense, chairman of the chief of staff, secretary of the navy, Medal of Honor Legion of the U.S., and the House Armed Services Committee.

The voice of Congress denies the charge of racial discrimination as being a part of the reason for not awarding Doris Miller the Medal of Honor. Some American war heroes have posthumously received the medal. Yet, of the 1.5 million black men who served, none have been awarded the Congressional Medal of Honor.

	DATE DUE	

13332

921 MIL Miller, Vickie Gail.

Doris Miller : a silent medal of honor winner

**LONGFELLOW ELEM SCHOOL
HOUSTON TX 77025**

785965 01096   32030D   008